MESSAGES FOR HEALTHY SELF-ESTEEM

HEALOGRAMS
▽
2

HOW TO LEARN TO LOVE YOURSELF

Bryan E. Robinson, Ph.D.
Jamey McCullers, R.N.

Health Communications, Inc.
Deerfield Beach, Florida

©1992 Bryan E. Robinson and
Jamey McCullers
ISBN 1-55874-205-0

All rights reserved. Printed in the United States of America. No part of this publication may be reproduced, stored in a retrieval system or transmitted in any form or by any means, electronic, mechanical, photocopying, recording or otherwise without the written permission of the publisher.

Publisher: Health Communications, Inc.
3201 S.W. 15th Street
Deerfield Beach, FL 33442-8190

Cover design by Andrea Perrine

Happiness is not tomorrow.
Happiness is now.

Anthony de Mello

MESSAGES FOR HEALTHY SELF-ESTEEM

HEALOGRAMS
SERIES 2

1. How To Feel Good In Relationships
2. How To Learn To Love Yourself
3. How To Boost Your Self-Esteem
4. How To Heal Your Inner Child

INTRODUCTION
How To Learn To Love Yourself

Many of us encounter barriers that block us from achieving self-esteem on life's journey. Removing and overcoming these roadblocks take action and effort, but they can be done. All of us want to feel good about ourselves. These *Healograms* — positive, healthy messages we send to ourselves — help us remove negative thoughts and feelings that stand in the way of healthy self-esteem.

If you are a people-pleaser, if you are driven by "shoulds," "oughts," and other shame-based messages, if you put everyone else's needs before your own, if you are living your life for everyone but yourself, *Healograms* can help you take positive steps for a more fulfilling life.

This booklet contains written *Healograms* on a variety of topics that can help you learn to love yourself. Reflect on each of the messages and silently apply it to your own life. Then become actively involved in the healing process as you write your own *Healograms*.

Healograms help us combat the old negative messages we got when growing up — the harmful thoughts that still blink in our brain like neon signs. They help us unravel ourselves from addictive relationships so that we can feel our own feelings, make our own decisions, be our own person and stand on our own two feet. They help us to achieve a higher quality of life and live it with a healthy self-esteem.

HEALOGRAMS

How To Learn To Love Yourself

1. Overcoming Feelings Of Isolation 1
2. Being Part Of The Solution, Not Part Of The Problem 5
3. Being In The Now 9
4. Owning Our Feelings 13
5. Honoring Others, Honoring Ourselves 17
6. Accepting Our Physical Bodies 21
7. Embracing Our Good 25
8. Recovering From Emotional Paralysis 29

9. Connecting With The Universal Human Bond 33
10. Practicing Patience 37
11. Letting Go Of Anger 41
12. Stopping The Destruction, Starting The Construction 45
13. Refraining From Being Critical 49
14. Building Our Integrity 53
15. Overcoming Self-Deception 57

Overcoming Feelings Of Isolation

So many times we isolate ourselves from life, afraid to live it. We are afraid to feel — afraid that people will hurt us, that something bad will happen, that people will laugh at us. We wall ourselves up, becoming even more unavailable to friends and loved ones. Our addictions take over in our isolation and we get involved in excessive drinking, overeating, overworking and unhealthy relationships to cope with our emptiness.

Social contact is important for our self-esteem. When we isolate ourselves from others, we become isolated from ourselves, for it is through others that we understand who we are. As we open ourselves to others, we are more open to ourselves. By putting ourselves "out there" we make a statement to ourselves and the world that we are available to be a friend and that we can face life unafraid.

When we isolate ourselves from others, we become isolated from ourselves; as we open ourselves to others, we are more open to ourselves.

2

Being Part Of The Solution, Not Part Of The Problem

So many times we are the problem in our lives. We go around whining that life has handed us such a raw deal. But that is all we do — complain. The energy it takes when we gripe and grumble goes nowhere and is unproductive. Our constant complaints, like snowballs gathering more snow as they roll downhill, become larger and more out of control.

Being part of the solution takes us out of the victim role and gives us freedom and direction. The next time we get bogged down with a problem, instead of looking for someone else to solve it, we can try to figure it out ourselves. Instead of wasting energy on blaming others, we can put negative emotions to positive use by working on a solution. Being part of the solution, instead of part of the problem, empowers us to feel better about ourselves.

Being part of the solution, instead of part of the problem, empowers us to feel better about ourselves and causes others to view us in a more positive light.

Being In The Now

Sometimes we have trouble accepting where we are in our lives. We say that our self-esteem will improve when we get to a certain point or when certain conditions are right in the family or on the job.

This is a way of living in the future and missing the present. If we're always waiting for conditions to be right for us to feel good about ourselves, our self-esteem will always be an illusion.

All we have is this moment, this second. We don't need outer conditions to define our inner condition. We need our inner condition to define our outer conditions. So no matter what our circumstances, *now* is the time to accept and nurture ourselves — not tomorrow or next week. Yesterday is gone forever and next week will never arrive. All we really have is now — this second, this moment.

No matter what our circumstances, now is the time to accept and nurture ourselves — not tomorrow or next week — because now is all we really have.

4
Owning Our Feelings

Sometimes we waste a lot of time blaming other people for our low self-esteem. Perhaps we blame it on a bad childhood or a negative love relationship. We may say, "It's all their fault. He ruined my life. She made me mad."

Blaming the way we feel on someone else is a cop-out. Nobody — no matter what they say and do — can make us feel anything unless we already feel that way inside. The minute that we accuse others for the way we are, we put our lives in their hands and permit them to be in charge of our feelings. No one can cause us to think, feel or act in any way unless we let them.

Facing our problems and owning them help us become responsible for our thoughts, feelings and actions. Accepting responsibility for our feelings, rather than blaming others, empowers us and our self-esteem improves.

Owning our feelings and actions helps us understand that, if we continue to feel low about ourselves, it's because we have refused to do anything about it.

5

Honoring Others, Honoring Ourselves

We can wish and fret and hope that others will change. "If only he would straighten up and fly right." "Why can't she see my side?" We become exhausted trying to get others to see our point of view or to convince them that our way is the best.

Trying to change others is exhausting. As long as we put our energies into trying to change other people, we are fighting a losing battle. We can always present our point of view and let it go at that. But constantly trying to change other people's personalities or ways of doing things is impossible.

The best way to change someone else is to change ourselves. Once we are able to let others be who they are — even when we disagree, disapprove or become disappointed — we have begun to change ourselves. When we know we have done all we can do and follow a "hands off" policy, we become content.

*T*he best way to change someone else is to change ourselves. Once we are able to let others be who they are — even when we disagree, disapprove or become disappointed — we have begun to change ourselves.

Accepting Our Physical Bodies

We only get one body in this go-around called life. Some of us try everything under the sun to change the flaws we see in ourselves. We purchase hair color, makeup, wigs and other cosmetic supplements, as well as diet to make us more physically appealing. We expend enormous amounts of energy and money trying to change our bodies;

we're always coming from a point of lack and discontent. We get one part in shape and then search for another flaw to fix.

It is important to accept our bodies. We can learn to accept our love handles and our bald spots. We can like our eye and hair color. We can affirm and express gratitude for our physical bodies just as they are. We begin to feel better about ourselves because, as we affirm our one and only body, we replace our external focus of lack and discontent with an internal focus of gratitude and self-acceptance.

We begin to feel better about ourselves because, as we affirm our one and only body, we replace our external focus of lack and discontent with an internal focus of gratitude and self-acceptance.

Embracing Our Good

When good things start to happen to us, those of us with low self-esteem feel we do not deserve them. Some of us are so accustomed to struggle and heartache that we are uncomfortable with profit and happiness. We may even try to sabotage our newfound goodwill because we feel unworthy of it.

Removing roadblocks starts with us. Rebuilding our self-esteem is like falling into a lake with rocks in our pockets. We sink to the bottom at first. But as we take one rock out at a time, we gradually rise higher and higher. Soon we reach the top and breathe fresh air again. We can begin to feel that we deserve good things by embracing the good that enters our lives. The more we welcome it, give thanks for it and expect it, the more will come because there is an unending supply.

Seeing ourselves truthfully includes acknowledging and embracing all the good things about ourselves.

8

Recovering From Emotional Paralysis

How many of us procrastinate for fear of starting out wrong? How many of us allow our fears to imprison us? We avoid speaking in front of groups for fear of saying the wrong thing or going blank. We avoid an art class for fear of not being as good as Picasso.

Emotional paralysis lurks beneath our procrastination and

avoidance of demanding situations. This comes from a fear of failure.

An obese man was instructed by his therapist to walk 20 minutes a day. He told her that if he couldn't run for four hours, it wasn't worth the time to put on his tennis shoes.

Acknowledging our fears and recognizing them as separate from us helps us get through any situation. Instead of running away, we walk directly into scary situations and grow from the experience.

Acknowledging our fears and recognizing them as separate from us helps us get through any situation so that, instead of running away, we walk directly into scary situations and grow from the experience.

Connecting With The Universal Human Bond

Sometimes we treat ourselves as if we're inferior to others. Other times we may act superior to them. Both attitudes stem from low self-esteem and both put us in a position of inequality with others.

The goal of healthy self-esteem is to break through the bonds of inequality to accept and love ourselves and others on an equal plane. We do this by relating on a feeling, human level — a level on which all of us are the same. We look beyond the human body and address the human spirit within us all. We face ourselves and others equally when we discover there is a universal human bond of feelings with which we can connect that does not have a hierarchy of better or worse.

We break the barriers to healthy self-esteem once we begin to think of ourselves as genuinely equal — not superior or inferior — to others in our lives.

We face ourselves and others equally when we discover there is a universal human bond of feelings with which to connect that does not have a hierarchy of better or worse.

Practicing Patience

Healing our self-esteem is not a "quick fix." It takes time and patience to change patterns that took a lifetime to establish. We must be careful not to become discouraged when our self-esteem doesn't improve fast enough for us. Our impatient need to rush the healing process can backfire, causing us to feel like a failure and our self-worth to drop even lower.

Healing our self-esteem occurs each day with practice as we grow in self-understanding. Patience is required because it doesn't happen on our time schedules. Faith that we will eventually be where we need to be in the healing process helps us develop confidence in ourselves. We learn to give ourselves credit for the tiny gains we make. We know that these small steps eventually add up to giant strides and our self-esteem is being healed gradually.

Patience and faith that we will eventually be where we need to be in the healing process help us develop confidence in ourselves, and we give ourselves credit for the tiny gains we make.

Letting Go Of Anger

Holding onto anger is a major roadblock to self-esteem. Over time it builds into resentments which eventually harm us physically and emotionally.

Sometimes we're afraid that if we give up our anger, we will unleash a groundswell of emotions like a bursting dam. The biggest fear of all may be that once the anger is gone, there will be nothing left of us.

But the more we try to control it, the more out of control it becomes. Harboring anger and resentment hurts no one but ourselves. By looking at anger in terms of energy use, we can have some choice in our lives. It takes more energy to continue to feel anger than it does to let it go. We can ask ourselves, "Do I want to expend this much energy on being angry at this person or do I want to resolve it and spend my energy somewhere to my advantage?"

The next time anger strikes we can weigh the amount of energy it takes to carry it and then decide whether to bear the burden or just let it go.

12

Stopping The Destruction, Starting The Construction

So many times when we make a mistake, we beat ourselves up for the smallest of errors. We treat ourselves in self-destructive ways by shame and guilt, compulsive worrying, losing sleep, overeating or excessive drinking.

It helps to weigh the enormity of the mistake. Did it harm someone? Was it an innocent mistake that all of us make as part of our human condition? Once we put our errors into perspective, we can stop the destruction and start the construction by asking what we can do to resolve the wrong, what we can do to prevent it from happening again and — most importantly — what we have learned.

We can never stop making mistakes, but we can use the experiences as lessons for improving our lives. As long as we live, we will make "mistakes" because there always will be lessons to learn.

We can never stop making mistakes, but we can stop destroying ourselves when we do and use the experiences as lessons for improving our lives.

Refraining From Being Critical

It has been said that the faults of others are like automobile headlights. They always seem more glaring than our own. An important step in self-esteem is when we no longer point out the mistakes of others but shine the light on our own. Criticism of others is a stumbling block to positive self-esteem because each time we criticize others, we tear ourselves down. We usually criticize people for things we do not like about ourselves. When we are critical of others, it distracts us from the things we need to work on in ourselves.

As we refrain from criticism, we can take the energy we put into criticizing others and put it to good use. Kind words and affectionate support can do more to heal self-esteem than any human medicine. We can become mindful of whether our words harm or heal. Do we use our opinions to judge and condemn or to uplift and support?

We can take the energy we put into criticizing others and put it to good use by working on our own self-esteem.

14
Building Our Integrity

How often do we justify our wrongdoing by downplaying it? We cheat on our taxes because everybody else does. We find some money and keep it because "finders keepers." Or we tell a little white lie because no one will ever know.

No one else may ever know but *we* will know and we have to live with ourselves. Integrity is the mirror of positive self-esteem. Our actions always reflect how we feel about ourselves. Even when we know we can get away with dishonest behavior, we find our integrity guiding our self-esteem.

Asking ourselves if what we say is consistent with what we do is a good barometer of our self-esteem. Do we preach one thing and secretly do another? Integrity is like a turtle's shell, protecting our inner self and helping us behave in ways that fit with who we are, so that we feel at ease deep within ourselves.

Even when we know we can get away with dishonest behavior, small as it may be, we find our integrity guiding our self-esteem.

Overcoming Self-Deception

It has been said that the first and worst of all frauds is to cheat oneself. Self-deception is the refusal to see things as they truly are, as we would if we looked through the objective eyes of an outsider. Self-deception keeps us stuck in low self-esteem. It causes us to deny ourselves the same kindness and self-respect that we give to and expect from others.

Self-insight lifts the fog of self-deception. It helps us take an honest inventory of deceptive thoughts and feelings that have prevented us from seeing our own inner wonder, creation and worth.

Today we can let go of the self-deception that has held us back and see ourselves as we really are. We can acknowledge both our strong points and areas for improvement. But we refrain from putting ourselves down and treat ourselves with the same respect we give others.

Self-insight helps us take an honest inventory of deceptive thoughts and feelings that have prevented us from seeing our own inner wonder, creation and worth.